IMAGES
of America

SWAMPSCOTT

Swampscott's history for many years has been tied to the sea and fishing. Rodney Douglas, Lime Douglas, and Chester Smith pull a Swampscott dory onto Blaney Beach in the 1890s.

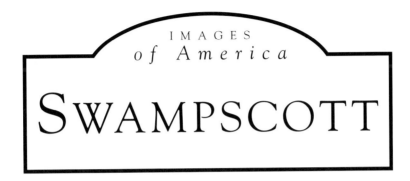

IMAGES
of America

SWAMPSCOTT

Kenneth C. Turino and Christopher R. Mathias

ARCADIA

First published 1996
Copyright © Kenneth C. Turino and Christopher R. Mathias, 1996

ISBN 0-7524-0521-7

Published by Arcadia Publishing,
an imprint of the Chalford Publishing Corporation
One Washington Center, Dover, New Hampshire 03820
Printed in Great Britain

Library of Congress Cataloging-in-Publication Data applied for

The town seal of Swampscott was adopted in 1881. It portrays the fishing schooner *The Dove* and owner James Phillips.

Contents

Acknowledgments

The authors are grateful to all those individuals and institutions that lent photographs to this publication and assisted with the research. Particular thanks must go to Louis Gallo, who fully supported this project by helping the authors acquire photographs and by supplying much-needed historical data. The town of Swampscott is fortunate to have such a knowledgeable historian. The staff of the Swampscott Public Library, namely Stephen Fulchino and Susan Zbinded, were extremely helpful and also supplied useful information. John Kobuszewski has generously lent images from his vast collections. Additional thanks go to Lil Limon and Arlene Kaufman of the North Shore Jewish Historical Society. The Lynn Historical Society and especially the Swampscott Historical Commission generously lent images from their outstanding photographic collections. Unless otherwise noted, photographs in this book are from the collection of the commission. Lastly, the authors wish to thank Fay Greenleaf who typed the manuscript and provided editorial assistance, and Borinous Schier and Ben and Sally Mathias for their encouragement and support.

Introduction

Picturesque Swampscott is among the earliest settlements in the United States. Originally settled in 1629, Swampscott was part of Saugust, whose name was changed to Lynn in 1636. In 1634, William Wood published *New England's Prospect* and described the area and the settlements of the Indians. One of these settlements was Swampscott, which meant "at the red rock." Although mainly a farming and fishing village, Swampscott is credited with the establishment of the first tannery in the Massachusetts Bay Colony; the industry belonged to Francis Ingalls, one of the original settlers in 1629.

As Lynn developed into an industrial center in the first half of the nineteenth century,

This idyllic view of Blaney Beach shows Lincoln House Point, and, in the distance, Little Nahant and a portion of Nahant, *c.* 1900. (Courtesy Lynn Historical Society.)

Swampscott maintained both a rural and maritime character. Eventually the village separated from Lynn, forming a town on May 21, 1852. A town government was established and the people began the process of building a town hall; originally meetings were held in the Atlantic Firehouse on Humphrey Street. The town also improved itself by purchasing a burial ground, establishing a fire department, developing schools, constructing roads, and bringing running water to the town.

Fishing had been the mainstay of the economy for many years, and the Swampscott dory was famous along the coast. But by the early 1880s, the fishing industry had reached its peak. With a scenic shoreline of over 4 miles and 3 sandy beaches, it was natural that Swampscott develop as a seaside resort. Easy access by train or trolley made it even more desirable as a resort. The wealthy, from cities like Boston, sought out the coast to escape from the cities' heat. At first many residents took boarders in their homes. Later elegant hotels and guest houses sprang up to cater to people on holiday and to take advantage of the views and beaches. The most famous hotel was the New Ocean House. Soon the very wealthy built gracious and grand homes and coexisted with the expanding middle class and the laborers, many of them Irish and Italian immigrants who came to work in the building trades.

For the town's 50th anniversary in 1902, Swampscott celebrated its accomplishments in high style with parades and fireworks. According to historian Frank Mansur, the "village of 1,000 people in 1852 had grown to a town of 4,600." Throughout this century, the town continued to grow and develop into the pleasant suburban community it is today. This book, through over two hundred photographs, many never published before, seeks to chronicle the growth of Swampscott from the 1880s up to the 1960s.

This scene of Fisherman's Beach shows why it was painted by artists such as Charles Woodbury and William Partridge Burpee.

One
Highways and Byways

This early morning photograph of 1889 shows Monument Square in the center and, to the left, Humphrey Street and Kings Beach. The trolley car barns can be clearly seen where Humphrey Street is cut off on the left.

This view of Blaney Street c. 1885 looks toward the 1854 Methodist church on Redington Street. The second building on the left is the 1846 Congregational church.

Monument Square and Burrill Street are shown here in 1889. Note the wall of the Mudge estate extending down Burrill Street. It was not until the early years of this century that the dual drives of Monument Avenue would be cut through the estate.

A horse-drawn trolley proceeds on a quiet Humphrey Street in the 1880s. The street would not be widened until 1914. (Courtesy Lynn Historical Society.)

This peaceful 1880s view of Orient Street looking west shows the Little Annawan hotel on the right.

Taken from Rockland Street looking toward Lynn in 1890, this photograph shows several prominent buildings. In the center is the Methodist church after its original spire was remodeled. To the right of this is the tall cylinder of the water tower, and to its right, the tower of the town hall. The spire to the left is that of the Congregational church. Above this and to the right is the long, low building that was the car barn for the horse railway.

This photograph of the house at 274 Puritan Road shows the street as a country lane instead of as a state highway. (Courtesy Lynn Historical Society.)

This view looking down Greenwood Avenue towards the harbor was taken in August of 1903. The small, low building to the right of the two girls is a ten-footer shoe shop, where shoes were assembled for the Lynn manufacturers. (Courtesy Lynn Historical Society.)

Children can be seen at play among the rocks at Blaney Beach. Humphrey Street runs behind the beach in this 1890s view. Note the building on the left, number 312, home of the Winnipesikett Club.

Orient Street with Orient Court running off to the left is captured c. 1900. Orient Street by 1905 was also called Puritan Road, the latter becoming the official name.

The ocean side of Humphrey Street at Blaney Beach contained these businesses in 1896-97. Later, the area would be named Chaisson's Park in honor of Lieutenant General John R. Chaisson (1916-1972), Chief of Staff, USMC.

The paving of Humphrey Street in 1914 caused the roadway to be closed to all but electric trolleys. The electrification of the car line was completed by February 1894.

Originally Paradise Road was just a woodland path dividing the Stetson and Redington Mudge estates. When this photograph was taken at the beginning of the twentieth century, whole stretches of woodland had still not been built upon. Soon groups that included the Stetson Land Company and the Swampscott Land Trust would develop the property.

Monument Square, formerly Mudge Square, is shown here in 1910. The land was given by the Mudge family for the purpose of erecting a monument to the fourteen soldiers who gave their lives in the Civil War. The granite monument with bronze trimmings and tablets rises 30 feet from the ground with a base 6 feet 10 inches square. It was dedicated in 1883.

This street scene looking into Monument Square shows one of the many small businesses along Humphrey Street. John Ralph's Boot and Shoe Repair Shop was in business between 1909 to 1911.

People stroll down Humphrey Street *c.* 1910. Boynton and Company at 218 Humphrey Street sold newspapers, stationery, books, and toys. (Courtesy John Kobuszewski.)

Stately houses along Humphrey Street face out on Blaney Beach in this 1912 photograph.

In the first decade of this century, Phillips Avenue consisted of a number of larger estates.

This street scene on Galloupe's Point was taken after a December snowstorm, capturing the peaceful beauty of the moment. (Courtesy Lynn Historical Society.)

Taken from the Phillips High School in 1913, this photograph looks down King Street. The steeple to the right of where the street ends belongs to the Methodist church on Redington Street; behind the church is the "new" Hadley School. The steeple on the left belongs to Saint John's Catholic Church. (Courtesy John Kobuszewski.)

This photographic postcard from the 1920s shows the boulevard along King's Beach looking toward Monument Square. Watts' Cafe was a popular destination for light refreshments. Later it became Grants' Cafe.

This Stuart P. Ellis photograph from the late 1920s is looking from Puritan Road to Humphrey Street. At this time, horse-drawn vehicles were still a common sight but the automobile was making great inroads.

Humphrey Street was hectic in the 1920s, as evidenced by this photograph. Cars line the street and bathers pack the beach.

Residents of Stetson Avenue took advantage of a sudden flood to go for a quick dip in 1924.

Puritan Road - Swampscott, Mass.

Puritan Road in 1924 was home to many summer residents like the Vorenberg family, whose house is to the right on Lincoln House Point. The family's winter residence was at 504 Commonwealth Avenue in Boston.

This 1930 shot shows Humphrey Street at the Phillips Beach railroad crossing. The Phillips Beach Fire Station can be seen on the right.

The corner of Greenwood and Bay View Avenues is shown here in 1946. The Phillips family home is seen to the left of the center with the high school behind it. The Phillips family owned most of the land in this area.

Humphrey Street is shown looking east from Monument Square in 1952.

This photograph of Monument Square in the late 1950s features the Civil War Monument. According to town historian Louis Gallo, the monument has been moved three times to accommodate changes in the street but never more than ten feet. Notice Doane's Restaurant, a popular eatery from the mid-1930s until 1975.

Two
Mercantile Pursuits

The Moose Hill Spring Water Company was one of several companies in Lynn and Swampscott specializing in spring water. The company was located at 42 Columbia Avenue and is shown here c. 1900.

The above view shows S.J. Pettingell's Grocery Store around 1890. Notice the drain pipe that supplied water to a cistern for water use within the building. By the 1922 view below, indoor plumbing had been installed. The men portrayed here, many in WWI uniforms, are from the American Legion, which meet in this building.

Mislabeled on this postcard as a factory, the Old Haskell Shop was actually a ten-footer shoe shop. The shoe trade started in Lynn and spread quickly through Essex County, where hundreds of shops like these were eventually established. Four to six men would work at low benches assembling shoes. (Courtesy Lynn Historical Society.)

This 1890s photograph shows the Albert G. Potter Box Company on Columbia Avenue at the Lynn line. The main building was actually in Lynn with out-buildings and Albert's home in Swampscott. (Courtesy Swampscott Public Library.)

Frank Griffin sits on his wagon in front of his carpentry shop at 43 Orient Street in this early-twentieth-century photograph. (Courtesy Mrs. Frank Griffin.)

This is the fish house of Thomas E. Stone, located on Humphrey Street opposite Greenwood Avenue, c. 1890. Mr. Stone was one of many Swampscott lobstermen; he lived at 39 Blaney Street.

George L. Chaisson, Boat Builders was located at 9 Elmwood Road. The company was in existence some time before 1916 and continued until 1954. An advertisement for the company stated that it was a "practical boat builder." George L. Chaisson made cabin cruisers, launches, skiffs, tenders, and all types of dories. This photograph was taken in 1925. (Courtesy Swampscott Public Library.)

The General Glover Inn was at one time home to the noted general. Lillian A. Little restored the building and operated it as a popular tea house for many years.

The Sunbeam Inn on the grounds of General Glover's Farm at Vinnin Square began life just after WWI as a little portable cottage to "give service through the medium of food, dancing and entertainment." By 1922 its overwhelming success resulted in the construction of this monumental building, which lasted till at least 1955. Later it lay derelict for many more years.

The tiled kitchen was hygienic and efficient, and had every modern labor-saving device. The Sunbeam prided itself in using the vegetables, eggs, milk, and small fruits from its own farm.

The gray fieldstone walls of the dining room are set off to advantage by the red imported tiles. The ceiling is a light blue and windows are draped with rainbow-colored fishnet curtains. The black lacquer furniture was complemented by fresh flowers from the Sunbeam gardens.

The second-floor dancing area known as the Rainbow Room had tinted walls decorated with grotesque flowers and birds in bright colors. Overhead hung colored and decorated canvases that lent a festive air. The room was lighted with ships' lanterns, which glowed red and green.

Humphrey Street at the corner of Redington in 1930/31 shows the variety of businesses to be found. At 146 Humphrey Street is Saint Clair's Restaurant (later the site of Eaton's Drug Store), which had branches in Hyannis and Boston. At number 154 was E.E. Gray's Grocery Store; at number 156, the George L. Rabinowitz import business; and at number 160, Young's Dry Goods. The next building contained Jeffers & Charles, Druggist; to its right was Saint John's Church. (Courtesy Swampscott Public Library.)

Town directory research shows that there were numerous restaurants along Humphrey Street that catered to visitors as well as the locals. Many of these restaurants lasted only a few years. Curtis's Restaurant, the interior of which is shown here, was located at 422 Humphrey Street in 1916 and later at 408-410 Humphrey Street. The restaurant had closed by 1922. (Courtesy Swampscott Public Library.)

Swampscott's commercial district is just a few blocks along Humphrey Street. In this photograph looking east we see George J. Herath's Pastry Shop, the Blaney Beach Market, the North Shore Barber Shop, Paradise and Varallo Shoe Repair, and the Blake Horological Studio. The "Hair Bob a Specialty" sign in the barber shop helps date this photograph to *c.* 1930. (Courtesy Louis Gallo.)

H. Allen Durkee and Fred L. Mower of Swampscott began making "Toot Sweet Marshmallow Fluff" and soon incorporated as Durkee-Mower in 1920. Their first factory can be seen in this Burrill Street photograph of 1924. Floods were a common occurrence here. (Courtesy Durkee-Mower Company.)

The New Ocean House complex included this structure, half of which was a parking garage and half a convention hall. In the top photograph people are leaving one of the two entrances, and in the bottom photograph the hall is hosting a dental convention.

The hall included space for exhibitors in this dental convention. Notice the many products dentists might purchase. Enamel and gold are prominently displayed.

Incorporated in 1903, the Tedesco Country Club has had a series of disastrous fires. The first building was destroyed in 1904 and replaced with the building shown here, which in turn was destroyed in 1932 by fire. The club takes its name from a rocky ledge off Little's Point where the barque *Tedesco* broke up in a blinding snowstorm. (Courtesy John Kobuszewski.)

The Holden Block was located at 128-136 Humphrey Street at the corner of Redington Street. George H. Holden's Grocery and Hardware Store dates from before the turn of the century and originally took up the whole block. By this *c.* 1938 photograph, the Parisian Dry Cleaning Company had taken over number 130. This company also had several locations in Lynn. The grocery store was out of business by 1940. (Courtesy Swampscott Public Library.)

Alphonse Chiancone operated his tailor's shop at 224 Humphrey Street at the corner of Blaney Street from the early 1920s for many years. Here we see the shop *c.* 1930.

This photograph was taken around 1945 and shows C.H. Martin's Fish Market at 424 Humphrey Street and the antique gift shop at 426 Humphrey. Martin's Fish Market was established in 1902; originally it was Martin and Durgin at 436 Humphrey. The fish market remained in operation until 1966. The gift shop began after 1942 and was gone by 1951. (Courtesy Swampscott Public Library.)

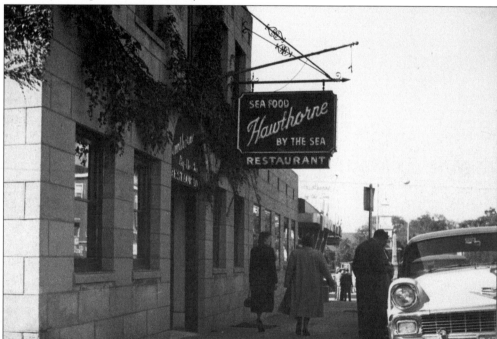

Anthony Athanas, son of an Albanian fruit peddler, rose in the restaurant business and eventually became a millionaire. His first restaurant, The Hawthorne Cafe, opened in Lynn in 1938. Hawthorne By The Sea, pictured here, opened in 1947. Ten years later, he acquired the General Glover Inn. (Courtesy Louis Gallo.)

Three
Summering by the Sea

The Lincoln House was built by S.H. Wardwell at the western end of Phillips Point and run for many years by the Wardwell brothers. This view across Blaney's Beach c. 1895 shows it to be a substantial establishment with excellent views from almost every vantage point. (Courtesy Lynn Historical Society.)

In 1864, E.N. Wardwell bought the "Beach House" and moved it from near the site of the Ocean House at Phillips Point to Whale Beach, renaming it the Ocean House. This photograph shows the building around 1880. Unfortunately, this also burned in 1882. (Courtesy Lynn Historical Society.)

The New Ocean House was built in 1884 and remained more or less unaltered until 1902.

In the 1890s, the Swampscott Hotel coexisted with fishermen's houses as well as fish shacks and dory rental yards on King's Beach. The combination of recreation and labor on the beach is revealed by the signs, "Bathing Rooms to Let" and "Surf Bathing Suits to Let," as well as the fishing nets laid out to dry in close proximity to the hotel. (Courtesy Lynn Historical Society.)

This family hotel in 1898 was called Big Annawan and was located on a knoll across from Tupelo Road. The name was later changed to the Oakland House.

The eastern facade of the Lincoln House is shown here in 1895. There was direct access to beach activities. In the 1780s, this cove became known as the "Shakers Bedroom" for the Shakers who came here from Canterbury, New Hampshire, during the warm weather. (Courtesy Swampscott Public Library.)

The cool ocean breezes refreshed guests lounging on the piazza of the Lincoln House. Galloupe's Point is in the distance. (Courtesy Louis Gallo.)

The Hotel Preston at 441 Atlantic Avenue was built in 1872. This 1926 scene demonstrates what a commanding view it had at Beach Bluff. The many piazzas allowed for leisurely relaxation while the changing rooms on the seawall let the more active guests enjoy the expansive beach.

The cottages at the Hotel Preston in this 1926 photograph indicate how the resort developed over time. These two buildings are as different in style as they are in age. The resort even had its own charging station for the electric cars guests might bring with them.

A turn-of-the-century advertising brochure for "The Cliff" states that it is only a seven-minute walk from the train station and a half-hour ride from Boston. "Situated on high ground with spacious lawns fronting the principal Boulevard, while in the rear one finds peaceful rest . . . only disturbed by the ripple of the sea as it beats on the adjoining beach. Perfect for those seeking a cool and quiet summer house." The resort was located on the current site of Saint John's parking lot.

The only way to get to the beach at the Cliff House was through this dramatic cleft in the rocks.

The Willey House at 80 Humphrey Street began as a boarding house in 1910 and after a hiatus of a few years in the late 1920s and 1930s it was transformed into a hotel and lasted until 1970. It ended its existence as the Sea Breeze Inn, which featured topless dancing. (Courtesy John Kobuszewski.)

The Deer Cove Inn was located on the former Phillips Estate at the corner of Puritan Road and Humphrey Street. Its quaint attractiveness was appreciated by middle-class people seeking a respite from the city. A riding stable was located nearby, where an English riding master gave lessons. In the 1930s, the town passed an ordinance forbidding stables in the area. Later the inn was sold and demolished to make way for house lots. (Courtesy Lynn Historical Society.)

The Hotel Bellevue at the corner of Crosman Avenue and Humphrey Street in the Beach Bluff section was a middle-sized hotel with full services including private bathhouses at the beach (a seven-minute walk). Putting their best foot forward, the management stated, "There are no beach resorts in this locality, so that the large and noisy crowds are wholly absent." This 1931 winter scene is one summer guests would shun.

The living room in the Bellevue was simply furnished and had a cozy fireplace and steam heat.

The dining room of the Bellevue accommodated all the guests with ease. "The manager maintains personal supervision over the culinary department with an efficient corps of cooks and servants, and aims to keep the table service always on a high plane."

The New Ocean House, shown here in 1929, was most certainly the Grand Dame of hotels in Swampscott. R.W. Carter of Boston rebuilt and reopened the Ocean House in 1884, giving the new establishment the less-than-original name of the New Ocean House. In 1895, the hotel was sold to Allen Ainslie and Edward R. Grabow; they installed electric call bells in all 175 rooms, a telephone, and an elevator. After a fire a few years later and another $100,000 in renovations, the hotel was reopened in 1902. As patronage increased, Ainslie and Grabow added an orchestra, concerts, dances, stables, vaudeville, and golf and tennis tournaments.

This panoramic view was taken from one of the upper floors of the New Ocean House. The hotel cottages are in the foreground, with Fisherman's Beach in the middle distance. Sailboats and fishing dories indicate some of the outdoor activities available. The Phillips School is on the hill to the right. In the far distance is King's Beach in Lynn.

In 1917 the fireproof Puritan Hall was added to the New Ocean House. The pergola in the front garden provided balance in the landscape and tended to lead the eye to the sea view. Obviously these young men and ladies have been distracted by concerns closer at hand.

The interiors of the New Ocean House were spacious and could accommodate many people. The hotel was the height of elegance in a New England seaside resort. The combination of wicker and overstuffed seating as well as hardwood floors and extensive carpeting made the lounge a very comfortable room to relax in. Note the classical columns that support the massive structure above, yet allow for an expansive interior vista.

Any meal was enhanced by the symmetry and opulence of the dining room. The interior dome with its foliar moldings opened up the space as no other architectural feature could. The stained-glass lighting fixtures and potted palms tie the two primary public spaces together. Even an extremely functional tile floor is made elegant by the contrasting design set into it.

50

Golf pro Mr. Cressey demonstrates a delicate shot in this 1920s vintage photograph. There were lessons offered daily, which attracted many sports enthusiasts. The course itself was thought to be the finest chip and putt in the area.

The evening also was devoted to entertainment. Performances by classical, jazz, and dance bands were very popular. One of the less high-brow evenings included the Silly Hat Contest. All hats had to have a theme. The elegant lady on the right in this 1956 competition has on a creation entitled the "Whole World in His Hands." Everyone might feel a bit foolish for a while but the event always drew many revelers.

In May 1969, the Swampscott Fire Department made a valiant attempt to fight the last fire to plague the great wooden ark.

Shown here are the remains of the once-great New Ocean House of Swampscott.

Four

Estates Grand and Small

This stone cottage was built for E. Redington Mudge and had a fine view of the ocean. It was entered from Burrill Street by a tree-lined avenue. Mr. Mudge moved to Swampscott from New Orleans in 1843 and purchased 130 acres including an old farmhouse. In 1863 he deeded the old house and 3 acres to his daughter and built Elmwood, which stood until 1955. This photograph of the estate was taken in 1940. (Courtesy Louis Gallo.)

Blaney House may have been built by Captain Ralph King on what became known as Humphrey Street near Black Will's Cliff. J. Blaney owned it by 1656. The house was razed shortly after this 1927 photograph was taken. (Courtesy Lynn Historical Society.)

This early stereopticon view shows the Stetson house. Colonel Charles A. Stetson owned the Astor House Hotel in New York beginning in 1837. This was his summer house at Woodside farm. (Courtesy Lynn Historical Society.)

The Mudge farmhouse is shown here before 1891 in its original location on Elmwood Avenue. It is thought to have been the original house of Lieutenant Governor John Humphrey. The Humphreys moved back to England in 1641, selling the 1,300-acre estate to Lady Deborah Moody. Thereafter the property was purchased by Ebenezer Burrill, whose family owned it until 1799. It passed through several owners until 1843 when Mudge acquired it. It was moved to Paradise Road in 1891 and is now the headquarters of the Swampscott Historical Society.

The water tower at Brier Gate, the residence of John Mason Little, is shown here. This estate was built in 1874 on a portion of the larger property owned by Little's father at Phillips Point, now known as Little's Point. This Shingle style tower and reservoir supplied all Little's cottages with water from a nearby spring. A steam engine pumped the water.

The General Glover homestead is shown here before it became the General Glover Inn. John Glover was a Revolutionary War hero from Marblehead and the first marine general. He faithfully served his friend George Washington to the detriment of his fortune. In later years, he moved to this farmstead in the part of Salem that was annexed to Swampscott in 1867.

The Burrill family house was a fine antique home located at the corner of Burrill and Essex Streets. Shortly after this 1924 photograph, Henry Ford bought and dismantled the home. It is thought that the materials were used in reconstructing other buildings at his museum, Greenfield Village, located in Dearborn, Michigan. The dining room mural was re-installed at the Wayside Inn in Sudbury, Massachusetts.

This photograph of Galloupe's Point *c*. 1898 shows the grand estate of Charles W. Galloupe. To the left of the house, notice what was probably a latticed clothes yard. This enclosure protected freshly-laundered items while drying as well as concealing unsightly daily chores. (Courtesy Lynn Historical Society.)

This stereopticon view taken before 1878 depicts the garden of Charles W. Galloupe's first house, which was destroyed by fire on June 2, 1880. The embellishments include a gazebo and a statue of Bacchus. To the right of the gazebo is a statue of a large domestic dog. (Courtesy Lynn Historical Society.)

A winter storm in the late 1880s or early 1890s is battering Head Rocks at the home of John Stanley. Located at 117 Humphrey Street, the homestead is directly adjacent to the west end of Blaney Beach. Even the working and middle class could enjoy the spectacular scenery.

In November 1906, Mrs. Willis Paul sent a postcard with a picture of her Gothic Revival house at 60 Redington Street. She described it as a "miniature 20 room mansion" and noted her mother was on the stairs and her daughter in front of the house. (Courtesy John Kobuszewski.)

Mary Baker Eddy lived at 23 Paradise Road from the fall of 1865 to the spring of 1866. It was here that Mrs. Eddy had her spiritual healing, which led to the discovery of Christian Science after her fall and injury in February 1866. The building is now a house museum run by the Longyear Foundation. (Courtesy John Kobuszewski.)

The Stephen H. Wardwell house is shown here in 1890. This rather simple late Victorian house has a solid, stable feel to it. There is very little surface decoration but the austerity is relieved by iron cresting over the second-story bay and balustrades above the porch. Saint John the Evangelist Church was built on adjoining property on Humphrey Street in 1904. In 1908, the church bought the Wardwell house and remodeled the interior for its rectory.

President and Grace Coolidge appear in front of White Court with their dog Rob Roy in 1925.

White Court was built for Frederick E. Smith of Dayton, Ohio, in 1895. President Calvin Coolidge used this home, owned by Wallace Falvey, for his summer White House in 1925. Coolidge gained access to the house through the influence of a neighbor, Frank W. Stearns, who was a close friend of the president.

A U. S. Marine encampment was staged at Lincoln House Point during President Coolidge's 1925 summer vacation.

Governor Gaston's summer home on Woodbine Avenue is featured in this shot. Gaston's sister Sadie is in the doorway and Constance Lewis Holt is with the bicycle. This house became one of the New Ocean House cottages and was razed with other hotel cottages. William Gaston was governor of Massachusetts from 1875-1876.

This two-and-a-half story Georgian Revival house, shown here in 1944, was built in 1889 for Professor Elihu Thomson, who was brought to Lynn by the shoe manufacturers to electrify the shoe factories. The exterior is finely detailed with a railing on the flat hip roof surmounted by urns, broken scroll pediments over the dormers, and a columned portico entrance. The Thomson-Houston Electric Company joined with Thomas Edison Company to become the General Electric Company. This house became Swampscott Town Hall in 1945.

This winter scene of the Thomson House shows the professor's observatory on the front lawn. Thomson constructed the 10-inch telescope himself and used it for thirty-five years, never missing a total eclipse. To the right of the observatory can be seen the E.R. Mudge house, in close proximity.

The elegant dining room of the Elihu Thomson House featured hardwood moldings, columns, and wainscoting. All the lighting fixtures, including these stained-glass examples, were the most modern to be found anywhere.

This post-1916 view of Lodges Cove and Tedesco Point demonstrates the dramatic beauty of the rocky coast that the summer residents so prized. In the center is Graystone Hall, the estate of Herbert E. Gale at 391 Puritan Road. To the left is the estate of Thomas Hunt, called Miramore. (Courtesy Lynn Historical Society.)

The Andrew W. Preston estate at 350 Atlantic Avenue consisted of 20 acres and several buildings. The house called The Arches was built in 1904 using a white brick and stucco exterior. The main living hall was two stories high with a balcony around the upper level that gave access to several bedrooms. This 1932 photograph shows how well it was kept.

Five
Rocky Ledges and Sandy Shores

Blaney Beach in 1884 was much closer to Humphrey Street. The horse-drawn transport has just delivered some crates but everyone pauses for a portrait before moving them further. The house in the center, built in 1785 by Joseph Ingalls, is now the Swampscott Club.

The beaching of three schooners on Fisherman's Beach was captured on a Wm. T. Webster stereopticon view in the 1880s. The curious were drawn to watch the scraping and recaulking of the hulls.

The Lincoln House had an intimate view of the harbor and town in the 1880s. The image at right was taken from a Wm. T. Webster stereopticon view.

Miss Greenwood seems justifiably proud of her elegant horses and carriage as she poses on King's Beach.

Benjamin Martin and son pose for a photograph in front of his lapstrake sailboat in this early 1890s view of Blaney Beach.

Whale Beach is shown looking toward the Ocean House from Lincoln House Point in 1884. In 1828 the Swampscott schooner *Hope* towed in and landed a large whale on this beach, and hence its name. (Courtesy Lynn Historical Society.)

This snowy scene at Black Will's Cliff at the end of King's Beach was a result of the severe winter storm of January 21, 1881. (Courtesy Lynn Historical Society.)

This charming artistic photograph of the early 1880s shows an early spring scene at Grasshead, the estate of James L. Little. (Courtesy Lynn Historical Society.)

This 1880s view looking west from the Ocean House shows Blaney Beach. Lynn and lower Swampscott are in the distance. (Courtesy Lynn Historical Society.)

This scene greeted guests gazing out their room windows at the Ocean House in 1881. Galloupe's Point is in the distance. The Little Annawan is the building in the foreground. (Courtesy Lynn Historical Society.)

This view, which looks southeast from the Ocean House in 1880, illustrates the panorama across Nahant Bay. Senator Henry Cabot Lodge's estate in Nahant is above the schooner's mast with Egg Rock to the left. (Courtesy Lynn Historical Society.)

This mid-1880s scene near the eastern end of Blaney Beach shows the size of the beach and Black Will's Cliff in the distance. (Courtesy Lynn Historical Society.)

This panoramic winter view around 1890 shows the sweep of Fisherman's Beach around to Lincoln House Point. Note the proximity of the Ocean House at the left and the Lincoln House on the point.

A class observes their art instructor on Fisherman's Beach just after the municipal fish house was completed in 1896. John Smith's Boat House is yet to be torn down. Charles Woodbury may very well be the artist, since he was known to have been working in the area at this time. Other artists painting along the beach included C.E.L. Green, Edward Burrill, E.A. Page, and Nathaniel Berry (all of Lynn), and William Patridge Burpee.

These girls are enjoying the beach on a hot summer day
sometime during the 1890s.

In a less environmentally-sensitive era, the capture of this porpoise at Blaney Beach drew a lot
of attention.

These men gathered for a portrait on the westernmost end of Blaney Beach in 1890. Fishing nets are hanging from the railing above the seawall. The man with the wagon is Timbo Barnes.

In this late-nineteenth-century photograph of King's Beach, you can clearly make out the monument and its proximity to the water. King's Beach is named for Daniel King, who owned much of the land bordering this beach in the mid-seventeenth century.

This electric trolley narrowly misses a breaking wave coming in from King's Beach around 1890. The seawall has yet to be completed and you can see the seaweed and debris washing right up to the street.

This turn-of-the-century view and the one to follow are both looking east from Whale Beach in front of the New Ocean House. Seagoing vessels have always been cautious of these craggy outcrops and some have not successfully avoided them. This photograph shows Jeffries Point and Inner Ledge. (Courtesy Lynn Historical Society.)

This view, also in front of the New Ocean House, shows Galloupe's Point and Dread Ledge.

This late-nineteenth-century photograph shows Black Will's Cliff at the eastern edge of King's Beach.

Phillips Beach is seen here c. 1900 directly below the Hotel Preston at Beach Bluff. The Swampscott-Marblehead town line is at the curve of the beach. The Bluffs were removed for fill at Logan Airport in the 1950s. (Courtesy Lynn Historical Society.)

This photograph was taken one stormy day at Black Will's Cliff. The cliff was named for the sachem of the local Indians in 1630, who was known as "Duke William" and locally referred to as Black Will.

This 1902 view of Blaney Beach from near the Lincoln House shows the new municipal fish house and many middle-class homes climbing the hillside. The Tudor style building is Pettingell's store across Humphrey Street. Note the animal pen to the left.

Dow's Rock at the eastern end of King's Beach on Black Will's Cliff was mainly residential in 1903. Today it is the site of Dale's Restaurant and Hawthorne By The Sea.

This unfortunate schooner is breaking up after being thrown onto the rocks off Galloupe's Point in 1914. One mast has snapped in half, the other trails alongside, and the hull is coming apart just forward of the cabin.

By 1926, Blaney Beach was taken over for recreational purposes on a hot summer day. The New Ocean House is on the right.

This rare 1927 photograph documents a film being shot on Whales Beach in front of the New Ocean House. Many onlookers have perched on nearby rocks to watch the action centered on the dory at the water's edge. (Courtesy Lynn Historical Society.)

This dramatic scene near the New Ocean House suggests a moonlight outing. Many photographic artists used the new technologies of the 1920s with great success. Lincoln House Point is in background. The hotel was renovated in 1922.

Six
Old Salts and Salt Cod

Partners Henry Leger and Ed Wiley split mackerel. Although one of the men had to walk with a cane, the two could still do a day's work. Transport is close at hand to take the cut fish up the beach to be salted.

The first Swampscott fishing schooners, called "jiggers," were fitted out in the 1790s. Before that there was only dory fishing. This 1890s workhorse off Galloupe's Point is underway, just having left the harbor. Note the dory on deck.

By the early 1880s, fishing at Swampscott had reached its peak; the fish houses at Blaney (Fisherman's) Beach in this 1884 photograph show much use. The boat owners are branching out, though. A small sign on the corner of the center building says, "Boat to Let. Party Boat Adina."

This 1895 view from the water's edge across the harbor to Lincoln House Point is noteworthy because it shows the diversity of fishing activities. In the foreground are beached dories. Men are occupied in their dories, sails furled and unfurled in the middle distance. On the horizon are schooners underway.

Fortunately, the noted Swampscott dory was light enough for one person to drag it up the beach while four able-bodied men observed.

A late-nineteenth-century photographer was able to convince a few of the fishermen to pose for informal portraits. Above is "Lum" Seger, and below is Solomon Abbott. The names of the fishermen to follow appear next to their respective portraits.

Mr. Hammond.

Nate Rich.

Rodney Douglas.

Pete Martin.

Children gathered on Blaney Beach on a summer's day to see what was going on. Someone has gotten dinner from the fisherman in the distance, while others are watching an artist at work.

Phil Crowley salts down the split fish.

Here we see two fishermen with pitchforks unloading their daily catch from the dory into a horse-driven wagon.

This young man is helping his father bring the nets up the beach in the horse cart.

These views show how the dory was brought up the beach with the use of two logs cut to the same diameter (in a process known as "rolling up the dory"). The well-known Swampscott dory had a great advantage over others. It was very wide in the middle, which made it a stable boat in rough water.

Charles Jones works on his lines. This fine 1890s photograph shows the post and moveable beam support that had multiple uses. We can see several masts with sails leaning to dry, baskets and anchors hanging, and nets airing.

This 1897 view clearly shows the split fish drying on racks at the beach. A cloth draped above the fish allows them to dry evenly and keeps birds and insects away. Note the tall framework on which to dry nets. (Courtesy Lynn Historical Society.)

The Fish House was built in 1896 by the town to replace the numerous individual fish houses. It is the only known municipal fish house in continuing use in the United States. The 1897 Report of the Park Commissioners states, "We have aimed at two things: A convenient and sanitary quarters and an architecturally attractive structure becoming of a high class pleasure resort." (Courtesy Lynn Historical Society.)

The non-fishermen were always drawn to the picturesque nature of fishing. Here, well-dressed men relax and watch the fisherman carrying out what he perceives to be a utilitarian task.

Fishermen and their children work to bring in a load of fish while the son of a summer resident leisurely looks on.

Captain Miles Blanchard sailed on many Swampscott vessels. In his youth he went to California during the 1849 gold rush but returned and continued fishing. He owned property where the Ocean House golf course and swimming pool later existed.

Captain Reuben Cary repairs a line. The wicker basket was a convenient form and shape in which to store and transport the hundreds of feet of line needed.

Edward Marsh looks very comfortable sitting in his beached dory whittling a replacement part.

Certainly an old salt if there ever was one, Captain Stanley appears in his rain gear in this 1889 photograph.

Seven

Our Community Life

The town's first appropriation for a fire department came in 1873 when the Atlantic, a hand-tub, was moved to new quarters on New Ocean Street. The Silsby steamer shown in front of the station was purchased in 1881, the date of this photograph. (Courtesy Louis Gallo.)

Although Swampscott became a town in 1852, it was not until 1860 that work began on a town hall at a cost of $4,381.43, including the land. Located on Burrill Street at the site of the present fire station, the town hall hosted its first town meeting on March 9, 1861. (Courtesy Lynn Historical Society.)

Swampscott's first high school was established in the town hall in 1876 and later moved to Redington Street. This class portrait was taken on May 25, 1885. In the center are Principal E.P. Barker and his assistant, S.M. Barker. (Courtesy Louis Gallo.)

The tower, bell, and clock were added to the town hall in 1885 and the ell on the east side was built in 1902. In 1960, the building was razed for the new fire station. (Courtesy Lynn Historical Society.)

The police department was photographed in front of the ell of the old town hall in 1903. The first police station was established here in 1865. From left to right are: (front row) Adebert S. Hammond, Chief Charles H. Dunlap, and John Whorf; (second row) Charles Connell, Joseph D. Spinney, and Samuel T. Harris.

The First Church of Swampscott, Congregational on Blaney Street was dedicated on July 15, 1846. The Reverend Jonas Bowen Clarke, a summer resident, initiated fund-raising for the building, and a Mrs. Weeks donated the land. This renovated version of the building was done in a handsome Romanesque Revival Shingle style.

This striking sunlit interior shot shows the main body of the First Church of Swampscott, Congregational as it was remodeled in the then-current high Victorian style. Notice the decorative stenciling on the wall, which accents the wainscoting and arched windows. (Courtesy Swampscott Public Library.)

The Swampscott depot is shown bustling with activity. In 1838, the Eastern Railroad opened a track that ran from Boston to Salem. The first passenger train came through the town on August 27. This depot was constructed in 1872.

On its way into Boston, a train is pulling into the depot. In 1895 the railroad grade crossing at Burrill Street was eliminated by the construction of an underpass which remains today.

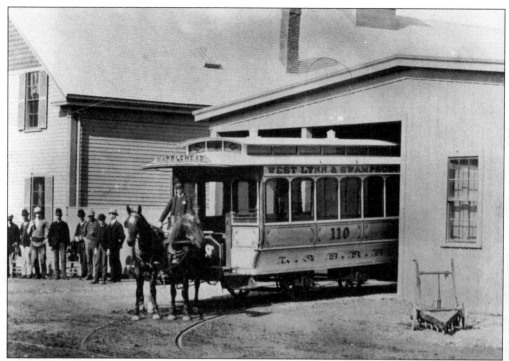

The Lynn and Boston Horse Railroad was extended to Mudge Square in 1881. It was expanded through Swampscott by way of Phillips Beach and Beach Bluff to Marblehead in 1884. The horsecar barns shown here were built on Humphrey Street near Stacey Brook that same year. (Courtesy Lynn Public Library.)

The horse-drawn Hook and Ladder #1 poses in front of the Central Fire Station on New Ocean Street. (Courtesy Lynn Historical Society.)

This photograph shows the fire department in November 1892, the year a new fire station, shown in background with its tower, replaced the old one on New Ocean Street.

The auditorium at town hall is all decked out for a Christmas celebration.

Steamer fire engine #1 speeds down Burrill Street in front of town hall en route to a fire in this rare view. (Courtesy Lynn Historical Society.)

The handsome Phillips Beach Fire Station with its shingled tower for drying hose was built to meet the needs of a growing town. Begun in 1902, the building was dedicated in 1903. Notice the sleigh to the right of the building and the surrounding farmland. (Courtesy Lynn Historical Society.)

A 1903 interior view of the Phillips Beach Fire Station shows Chemical No. 1. (Courtesy Lynn Historical Society.)

The Phillips School, built in 1894, became the town's high school, which since 1876 had been in town hall. At first the school was also used by elementary students. In 1936, the building lost its tower and two wings were added; a third wing was added in 1966 and the building became a junior high in 1977 and a middle school in 1994. (Courtesy Lynn Historical Society.)

In 1911 an enthusiastic group of young women at Phillips High School formed the first girls' athletic association for the promotion of basketball. The 1913 season, under the direction of coach Jessie MacDonald, saw the team become the acknowledged state champions.

Saint John's Church on Humphrey Street opened for services on Christmas Day in 1904. Originally a mission of Saint Joseph's in Lynn, it became a separate parish in 1906. In 1908, the Stephen Wardwell estate adjoining the property was remodeled into a parish house.

This interior view of Saint John's Church was taken in 1913. The Humphrey Street location was actually its second; originally the church stood on Elmwood Road. (Courtesy Louis Gallo.)

This *c.* 1900 photograph is labeled "Highway Department;" it shows the workers taking time out from their Burrill Street job for a photograph. Shown here from left to right are: Mike Ryan, Michael Haley, Timothy Ryan, Dan Kane, Peter Coan, Dick Cobb, and John Champion.

Never one to hurry, the town of Swampscott after ten years of debate elected a board of sewer commissioners in 1900. It was not until March 1902 that the commissioners would begin construction of a sewer system, since the town had not appropriated any funding. This photograph taken during the summer of 1902 shows the construction on Humphrey Street. (Courtesy Louis Gallo.)

Well-known photographer Stuart P. Ellis captured workers laying wooden brick for Humphrey Street by Ingall Terrace. Shown here from left to right are two Ingalls family homes and the Swampscott Club. Notice the street railway tracks in this c. 1920 photograph.

The Central Fire Station on New Ocean Street replaced one of the original firehouses on the site in 1891. Five horses were purchased to haul the apparatus and were rented to the highway department to earn their keep. (Courtesy Louis Gallo.)

The Andrews Chapel in the Swampscott Cemetery on Essex Street was built with money donated by the late Ellen E. Andrews in memory of her husband, Isaac H. Andrews, a member of the board of selectmen in 1880 and 1883 and the board of assessors from 1880 to 1885. Designed by Charles V. Burgess, the Norman Gothic granite building was completed in 1924. (Courtesy Louis Gallo.)

The Hadley School replaced the Old Redington Street School in 1911. The school was named after Eloise J. Hadley, a popular teacher at the previous school and library trustee for forty-five years. The building has at various times housed elementary and junior high students.

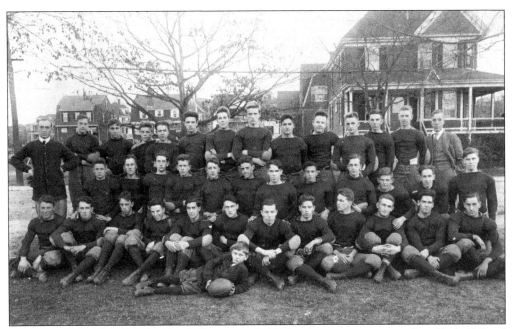

Swampscott High School's football team of 1915 takes time out at the Clark School Playground, later renamed Abbott Park Playground. At that time games were played in this park.

This youth group of the First Church of Swampscott, Congregational could not quite stay still for this 1920s Stuart P. Ellis photograph.

This structure at the corner of Burrill Street and Rock Avenue was originally home to the Baptist church in 1873. The Church of the Redeemer, Methodist purchased the property in 1923 from the Improved Order of Red Men. It was photographed shortly after this time. (Courtesy Swampscott Public Library.)

In 1852, Dr. William R. Lawrence of Boston gave the town 166 books and $100 as the basis for forming a library. Originally a subscription library was formed which lasted nine years. In 1866 a room of the town hall was set aside for the library and it remained there until this building was constructed in 1915 on Burrill Street. This photograph was taken before the new addition was added in 1956. (Courtesy Swampscott Public Library.)

The Beach Bluff station of the Boston & Maine Railroad was located on Beach Bluff Avenue. Closed in 1960, the station was demolished in 1961. (Courtesy Louis Gallo.)

This photograph taken in Jackson Park shows the members of the Civil Defense Force in the late 1940s or early 1950s. In these years, units were maintained because of the perceived threat of communism. (Courtesy Louis Gallo.)

The Swampscott Police Department is shown here c. 1926, just after the infamous "Rum Running Scandal." Swampscott had, according to the town documents, "become a habitual landing place for rum runners who operated without any genuine interference on the part of the police." The result was the firing of the chief of police and the reorganization of the whole department.

Marblehead High School, Swampscott's traditional rival, is defeated 13 to 0 in this 1946 game. In this action photograph, Ed Burke is making the tackle, Fran Cassidy is captured in the air, and Jack Dedbrick is coming up fast. (Courtesy Louis Gallo.)

The Swampscott High School hockey team of 1952 was coached by Ty Anderson, pictured here on the extreme right.

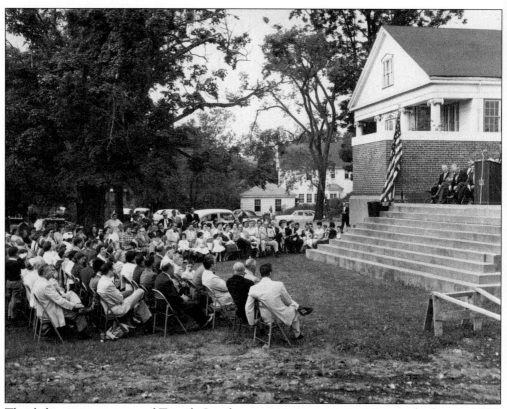

The dedication ceremony of Temple Israel, a conservative congregation, took place in 1956. Formed in 1946 with plans for a house of worship and a religious school for the fast-growing Jewish community, the temple purchased the Palmer-Ingalls estate on Humphrey Street. Notice the original Ingalls house with the Greek Revival columns and the construction of the stairs of the original temple, which was later redesigned as the present structure. (Courtesy North Shore Jewish Historical Society.)

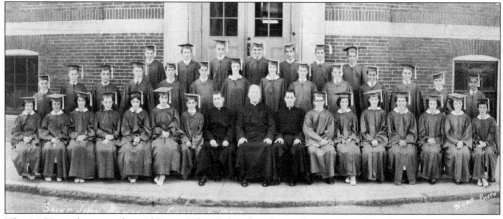

The 1957 graduating class of Saint John School is shown here. Seated in the center from left to right are: Father Cidron, Monsignor McDonough, and Father Mansfield. Noted Swampscott historian Louis A. Gallo is the last boy on the right in the second row.

Engine No. 2 is pictured at the Phillips Beach Fire Station. A Seagrave pumper is shown with two proud firemen. The engine was built in 1936, became No. 4 in 1955, and was eventually sold in 1975. (Courtesy Lynn Historical Society.)

The religious school of Temple Israel has always played an important role in the life of the temple. Here in the 1950s, children take part in the Chanukah celebration. (Courtesy North Shore Jewish Historical Society.)

The Phillips Beach station on the Boston & Maine Railroad is seen looking east in the 1950s. The station was razed on October 19, 1962. (Courtesy Lynn Historical Society.)

The baseball team of the Leon Abbott Post 57 of the American Legion at 89 Burrill Street poses for a group portrait in the early 1960s.

Eight
Not Business as Usual

The 50th Anniversary of the Swampscott Club was celebrated in July 1915. Members and guests are seated in front of the flag- and bunting-draped building watching the boat races across the street.

Samuel J. Pettingell's grocery store at 380 Humphrey Street was patriotically decorated for the celebration of the 50th anniversary of Swampscott. The event was met with much jubilation on July 21, 1902. There was a sunrise firing of guns and ringing of bells, a parade at mid-day, and concerts and fireworks in the evening. Note the flag of Teddy Roosevelt.

The corner of Humphrey Street and Greenwood Avenue is gaily decorated. The plumbing shop of Philbrick & Pope is on the left; we can see a toilet proudly displayed in the front window.

There were dozens of floats for the celebration. This one, built on a truck, had a history theme. Represented are exploration, discovery, colonization, liberty, and peace.

The Little Annawan hotel on Orient Street east of the New Ocean House is well-dressed with bunting. Dignitaries in summer white are parading in horse-drawn carriages. (Courtesy Lynn Historical Society.)

The Woman's Club featured a Colonial tableau on a horse-drawn cart. (Courtesy Swampscott Public Library.)

The Winnipesikett Club, incorporated on January 23, 1899, and located at 20 Rock Avenue, paraded in high fashion. Later the club would move to Humphrey Street. (Courtesy Swampscott Public Library.)

The Grand Army of the Republic veteran's association was active in town for many years. The General James L. Bates Post, No. 118, Swampscott, as it was known, was formed in the town hall on February 2, 1870. Here we see the GAR members showing the colors in this turn-of-the-century photograph in front of the main train station.

A Memorial Day parade of 1908 passes the corner of Burrill Street and Railroad Avenue. Most of the police are carrying bouquets of flowers to be deposited on the graves of Civil War veterans.

Colonial pageants were common in the early twentieth century, a fact to which this photograph attests. There was great interest in the Colonial period as the country became more industrialized. Notice the town seal prominently displayed behind the unidentified group on the stage of the old town hall auditorium. (Courtesy Lynn Historical Society.)

Not every event was a cause for celebration. During World War I, 511 Swampscott men enlisted with 12 casualties. Here the bodies of Elmer Bolunder and John Enos Blocksidge are laid in state at the town hall. The guard of honor included John Lee, Earl Jenkins, Jeff Seaton, and George Place.

The auditorium of the Hadley School was the setting for a victory garden display in the fall of 1918.

The toboggan shoot in Jackson Park is shown looking down at Essex Street *c.* 1920. Built in the early part of this century, the toboggan shoot was popular among residents as this photograph shows.

The dedication ceremony of Abbott Park on Paradise Road took place in the 1920s. The Abbott Park Boulder was erected in memory of Leon E. Abbott, who was killed in action at La Croisette, near Chateau-Thierry, France, on July 13, 1918. The bronze cross and plaque were copied from Abbott's grave marker in France.

The American Legion show of 1929 must have been a comedy, but its theme is lost to history. Five of the men are dressed in women's clothing. Does Louise Linden (first row, third from right) look amused by her husband who stands above her? The legion was noted for its theatrical productions and musical reviews. (Courtesy Swampscott Public Library.)

The Swampscott Yacht Club, organized in the 1930s, is headquartered at the Fish House on Humphrey Street. Here we see the club's youth group in 1937.

This Memorial Day parade of 1948 was blessed with fine sunny weather. The WWII vets march proudly on Humphrey Street in this patriotic era. Notice the long-lived Philbrick & Pope plumbing businesses in the background, as well as Eden's Restaurant.

This promotional photograph was taken at Hood's Cherry Hill Farm for Temple Israel's 1948 Country Fair. The committee members are, from left to right: (front row) Nellie Butman and Gert Zaiger, posing with an unnamed four-footed friend; (back row) Natalie Frisch, Sylvia Dine, and Chairman "Hy Karp." (Courtesy North Shore Jewish Historical Society.)

Santa—alias Giacomo (Jack) Gallo—makes an appearance at the new veterans housing on Cherry Street in the early 1950s.

The high school marching band passes Bickford's Pharmacy at 135 Burrill Street during the 100th anniversary parade on June 21, 1952.

On June 19, 1954, more than 1,500 people witnessed a hose-laying contest and an old-fashioned muster. The event was sponsored by the Swampscott Auxiliary Fire Department at Jackson Park. (Courtesy John Kobuszewski.)

Bibliography

Anderson, Dorothy M. *The Era of the Summer Estates Swampscott, MA 1870-1940*. Canaan, NH: Phoenix Publishing, 1985.

Garland, Joseph E. *Boston's North Shore*. Boston, MA: Little, Brown and Company, 1978.

Garland, Joseph E. *Boston's Gold Coast*. Boston, MA: Little, Brown and Company, 1981.

Lynn Suburban Directories. Salem, MA: Henry M. Meeks Publishing.

Mansur, Frank L. *Fifty Years of Swampscott Schools 1852-1902*. Swampscott, MA: Swampscott Historical Committee, 1969.

Mansur, Frank L. *Swampscott: The Beginning of a Town*. Swampscott, MA: Swampscott Historical Committee, 1972.

Standard History of Essex County Massachusetts. Boston, MA: C.F. Jewett & Co., 1878.

"Swampscott: One Hundred Years a Town." Official Centennial Book and Program. Swampscott, MA, 1952.

Swampscotta. High School Yearbook. Swampscott, MA, March 1952.

Thompson, Waldo. *Sketches of Swampscott*. Lynn, MA, 1885.

Warnock, Donald. *The Elihu Thomson House*. Swampscott, MA: Swampscott Historical Committee, 1978.

In the winter of 1954, members of Temple Israel staged a fund-raising show appropriately titled *Raisin Dough*. (Courtesy North Shore Jewish Historical Society.)